The Dumbfounding Confusion

IS
IDAHO
IN
IOWA
?

TIM WOODWARD

Backeddy Books
Box 301
Cambridge, Idaho 83610

To Mom,

Christmas, 1992

Love,

Tim

ISBN 0-9603566-8-1

FOREWORD

Why a book about Iowa-Idaho?

With respects to people who climb mountains, because
it's there. Mixups between these two states are so common
as to be almost unbelievable, which is why it seemed
reasonable to document some of the confusion and get it
between covers.

Believe it. It's real.

More than a decade has passed since a reader sent me my
first sample of Iowa-Idaho confusion. Oblivious to the
power of the phenomenon, I unwittingly used it as an item
in my column in the *Idaho Statesman* in Boise. It inspired
other readers to send their stories; soon there were enough
for an entire piece on the subject. From then on, the Iowa-
Idaho connection assumed a life of its own. At one time,
the file of unused material weighed in at nearly five
pounds.

Because many of the stories tend to sound alike — Iowa
potato yarns wear thin after the first ten or fifteen tellings
— it wasn't possible to use them all. The examples in this
book, a fraction of the whole, are offered as a representative sampling.

If more are from Idaho than Iowa, it's for reasons that
are fairly obvious. I'm an Idahoan. I was living and working in Idaho when they were sent to me, usually by Idahoans. Iowans and their stories have been included to the
extent possible, but Idaho still has the edge. The imbalance
is due to the constraints of geography and in no way is
meant to slight the residents of the fair state of Iowa.

As the title implies, Iowa and Idaho are the primary
victims of the confusion. They are by no means the only

ones, however. Indiana, Ohio, and even the mythical states of Idawa and Ohido share in the chaos.

An exaggeration?

Turn the page. Read. Believe.

Most of all, have fun. That's the whole point of an exercise like this. To borrow from Mark Twain, anyone taking the contents of this book seriously will be prosecuted. Anyone taking offense will be shot. Anyone attempting to find an ulterior motive will be banished to Merrill Sterler's hog lot.

Tim Woodward
April, 1992

CONTENTS

IT ALL BEGAN ...

Idaho and Iowa are states so different from each other it would seem impossible to confuse them.

Idaho is mountains, irrigated farmland, and desert. The definition of an Idaho rainstorm — a lot of wind, a lot of dust, a few drops and it's all over — is harsh but accurate. Travelers on the interstate that traverses the southern part of the state can be forgiven for thinking, with Thomas Wolfe, that Idaho is "an enormous desert bounded by infinitely faraway mountains that you never get to ..." Those who leave the interstate, however, will see alpine lakes, national forests, the nation's largest wilderness outside of Alaska, more than one hundred and fifty peaks higher than 10,000 feet. The highest is Mt. Borah, elevation 12,662 feet.

Iowa is flat, a textbook Midwest prairieland of thriving crops, fat livestock, and neat-looking farmhouses. Its endless expanses of greenery are the legacy of rich soil, abundant rainfall, and modern agricultural methods. It is possible to drive forever in Iowa without losing sight of a cornfield. The state has no national parks or forests. Its highest point is Merrill Sterler's hog lot, elevation 1,670 feet.

The two states are separated by a distance greater than that separating New York from Georgia. One is so flat that people in Sioux City communicate with residents of Dubuque, three-hundred miles away, by standing in the road and waving. The other is so mountainous that if pounded flat, according to some authorities, it would be the largest state in the nation. One is famous for corn, the other for potatoes — products not noted for striking similarities.

There is no compelling reason for people to confuse Idaho and Iowa, but they do. It happens somewhere in the English-speaking world approximately every thirty-six seconds.

Almost all of the mixups are funny; some border on the unbelievable.

At least one victim actually moved to Idaho, thinking it was Iowa. This really happened. He discovered his 1,500-mile error too late and has been an Idahoan ever since.

In Hawaii, a prospective thief was foiled by a geographic faux pas printed on his checks — drawn on the First National Bank of Iowa, in "Boise, Iowa."

He was in good company. In a golden moment from his reporting days, ABC anchorman Tom Brokaw ended a newscast with a panoramic sweep of the mountains of the Boise Front and the words, "This is Tom Brokaw reporting from Boise, Iowa." Not to be outdone, Deborah Norville stumbled over Boise, Iowa, a decade later on the Today Show.

The Boise, Iowa, syndrome has been the undoing of countless mail-order customers, including a couple who reported that "it took three months to get our order. The company kept sending it to you-know-where. When we told them we were from Boise, Idaho, they asked how far that was from Council Bluffs."

Answer: about fourteen-hundred miles, give or take a spud cellar or two.

Idaho is rife with ski resorts, including Sun Valley, the nation's first. Iowa's terrain is more conducive to lawn tennis. The difference in terrain, however, was not enough to stop the journal of the American Association of Retired Persons from plugging Iowa ski packages, or *The Wall*

Street Journal from moving Sun Valley to the Hawkeye State.

No one is immune. *Harper's* magazine, *Time, The New York Times,* even the President of the United States have succumbed to Iowa-Idaho madness. A sizable contingent of Americans, including members of the White House staff, believe that all four of the "I" states are in a neat line in the Midwest. Thus we have a hundredth-birthday card from George Bush to a resident of Emmett, Idaho — mailed to his correct street address, in "Emmett, Indiana."

Indiana is the state second most frequently confused with Idaho, followed closely by Ohio, which doesn't start with an "I" but has a similar sounding name. This was the inspiration for the old New Yorker joke about the Idaho woman who was visiting the East and was told, "My dear, I'm sure you won't take offense if I tell you something you ought to know. *We* pronounce it Ohio."

The University of Iowa does a respectable business in T-shirts printed with the words, "University of Iowa, Idaho City, Ohio."

This book is a partial compilation of the confusion, with individual incidents arranged according to categories that seemed to make sense. (A complete compilation is impossible, as the insanity is ongoing.) Anything resembling scholarly intent has been fiercely avoided. The only justification for a book like this is to have fun. Do not under any circumstance put it on your coffee table. The author respectfully suggests the nightstand or the bathroom.

We'll get to the incidents themselves shortly. First, a bit of history.

How and when did it all begin?

The first explorers to travel from Iowa to Idaho were members of the Lewis and Clark Expedition. As the states were yet to be named, it's doubtful anyone confused them.

Six decades later, in the most famous Oregon Trail incident involving Iowans in Idaho, the J. Hunter party of Iowa City advanced relations between the states by coming to Idaho and being slaughtered by Indians. The site of the 1862 ambush is now Massacre Rocks State Park.

How many Iowans came to Idaho in the years immediately following the Hunter incident is unrecorded, but it's reasonable to assume that it tended to depress emigration. That significant numbers of Iowans bothered with Idaho at all after the massacre was the result of the presidential election of 1884.

That was the year Grover Cleveland was elected President. According to Peter Harstad and Michael Gibson in an "Idaho-Iowa" article in *The Palimpsest,* Cleveland was the first Democrat to enter the White House in a quarter-century, and Iowa's Democratic newspaper editors were so delighted they went with him, so to speak. A group of a hundred and seventy-five visited the new President in the nation's capital in June of 1885.

Not to be outdone, the state's Republican editors decided to take a trip, too. (Then as now, journalists love nothing better than a good junket.) As an alternative to staying home and watching the corn ripen, the Republican editors opted to visit the Pacific Northwest, including what would become, five years hence, the new state of Idaho.

The trip was billed as "the Great Excursion of the Decade." It also was one of the great freebies of the decade. The Union Pacific Railroad had just completed construction of its Oregon Short Line across southern Idaho. The run included a spur line to Ketchum, a mile from what would later become Sun Valley.

Being astute businessmen, the railroad's directors had great respect for the power of the press — particularly if it included glowing travel articles about their newly opened territory. Accordingly, they offered the editors one of their best trains and the services of highly placed company officials at a cost of less than $20 per person. Being easy, the editors accepted.

Harstad and Gibson's account further reveals that Union Pacific's faith was not misplaced. One editor wrote that "a finer grazing country could scarcely be found than this part of Idaho." At Soda Springs, Idaho, the visitors predicted that "a few years will see a great sanitarium, with crowds of invalid visitors located at this point." In the Portneuf River Valley, they noted that the scenery was "very fine with beautiful cascades and waterfalls on the one side and enchanting mountains, frequently plentifully powdered with snow, and long dark canyons on the other." Prairie dwellers, one editor bubbled, "must see with their own eyes before they can have an adquate conception of (Idaho's) grandeur."

Idaho's Shoshone Falls were "far more pleasing and beautiful" than Niagara. "Having beheld the one, you do not rest until you have seen the other." In the mining town of Ketchum, lead and silver were "thrown around carelessly as bricks around a drying yard, and quartz and galena (lay) in great bins like corn in a Hawkeye elevator."

Mindful of their agricultural readership, the editors reported that Idaho's "horses, cattle and sheep look fat and sleek ...," and that "the small amount of grass contains a far greater percentage of the flesh-producing element than the native grasses in the states."

A Council Bluffs editor with a deft touch for irony observed that "sage brushes cannot grow except in rich soil." In the rich soil of the Idaho promised land, "Apples, peaches, pears, nectarines, apricots, plums, prunes, grapes and all the small fruits are produced in abundance, and of a quality your correspondent has never seen surpassed."

The result was inevitable. By 1890, Iowa was supplying Idaho with more residents than all but three other states. By 1900, it was third, behind Missouri and neighboring Utah. By 1910, only Utah exceeded Iowa as a source of new Idahoans.

In other words, the hordes who continue to confuse Idaho and Iowa today may not be quite as blockheaded as they seem.

Iowa's political influence on Idaho was astonishing. In a little over a century of statehood, no fewer than nine Idaho governors have hailed from Iowa.

And they've heard all the jokes.

You haven't?

On with the fun.

UP CLOSE AND PERSONAL

The scene: a service station in South Carolina.

Georgia traveler - We'll be home soon. Where is your home?

Idaho traveler - Boise, Idaho.

Georgia traveler - Well, now! I don't rightly know if we come through there or not. We come through St. Louis.

Idaho traveler - You probably didn't come through Boise then. It's two-thousand miles from St. Louis.

Georgia traveler - It is?!

Idaho traveler - It's less than a day's drive from the Pacific Ocean. Idaho isn't in Missouri. It's in the Wild West.

Georgia traveler - (backing up, checking for tomahawks) Start the car, Billy Ray. And don't make any sudden moves!

The story, with modest embellishments, is true. It happened to Idahoan Betty Burke in 1986. The Georgians, of course, were wondering whether they had come through Boise, Iowa. Americans have a continuing problem with Boise, Iowa.

And Des Moines, Idaho, and Coeur d'Alene, Iowa, and Sioux Falls, Idaho, and ...

No offense to Georgia, but the state of geography appears to be in serious trouble there. Lynn Adams of Red

Oak, Iowa, was traveling in the Peach State when one of the natives asked the inevitable question:

"So, where do you call home?"

"Iowa," she replied.

"Iowa. Let me see now. Wait, I've got it! That's the one up there by Washington and Oregon, isn't it?"

Adams is living proof that *The New Yorker's* provincial-easterner cartoon was based on real life:

"After many conversations with people from other parts of the country — each not knowing where Iowa was — I was talking to a gentleman who asked the usual question," she said. "He wanted to know where I was from. I told him I was from Iowa."

"Really? Here we pronounce it Ohio."

In 1989, the Idaho Falcons soccer team toured the now defunct Soviet Union, competing in Russia, Moldavia, and the Ukraine.

It was the first time a U.S. amateur soccer team had been invited to play in the U.S.S.R. The Idahoans were understandably proud to be representing their country — until they arrived in the stadium in Moscow for the last game of their tour.

Among the spectators was a Russian high school student with a hand-painted banner: "Go Iowa!"

No one could convince him there was a difference.

Back in the USSR?

Iowan Diane Foster claims the confusion is "always in favor of Idaho. They've heard of it, but not Iowa."

But fellow Iowan John Rowland swears that "most people think Idaho is in the USSR."

And Robert Mondt, a junior high school teacher in Red Oak, Iowa, pinpoints Idaho's location as "the third island in the chain of islands near the state of Hawaii."

Lyman Larson became so accustomed to seeing people mix up Idaho and Iowa he decided to have some fun with the confusion. His contribution? An Idawa postcard.

"Why do Idaho and Iowa have such an identity crisis?" he asked. "What is it that makes a person confuse them? Is it their geographic proximity, renowned rivers, or perhaps their famed agricultural products? In honor of confused fellow countrymen everywhere, I designed the appropriate postcard. It is my hope that it will simplify the confusion, or just simply confuse."

The postcard pays homage to "Idawa, the Gemeye State." Idaho's official name is the Gem — not potato — state; Iowa, of course, is the Hawkeye state. (The name honors Chief Blackhawk, who led two Indian tribes against whites in the Blackhawk War of 1832. He lost, of course. If he'd beaten the sodbusters, you can bet they wouldn't have nicknamed the state after him.)

Larson's postcard Idawa bears an uncanny resemblance to Iowa, with Idaho's panhandle jutting from its northern border. Its capital is Des Boise. The fifty-first state is the home of "Famous Corntatoes," and is modestly described as "a Pacific Midwest paradise bordered by the mighty Snake and Mississippi rivers."

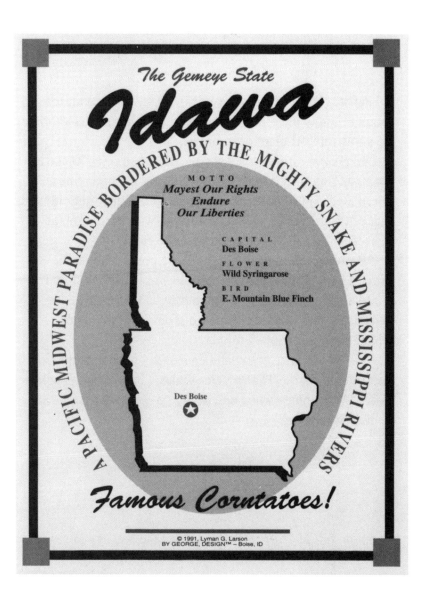

The Gemeye State

Idawa

A PACIFIC MIDWEST PARADISE BORDERED BY THE MIGHTY SNAKE AND MISSISSIPPI RIVERS

MOTTO
*Mayest Our Rights
Endure
Our Liberties*

CAPITAL
Des Boise

FLOWER
Wild Syringarose

BIRD
E. Mountain Blue Finch

Des Boise
★

Famous Corntatoes!

Patricia Roderick, a native of Indiana, married an Idahoan in Idaho and, later in the year, took her husband home to show him off at an open house.

"In northwest Indiana," she recalled, "an open house is a popular way to celebrate events. During the open house, I circulated continually, as a good guest of honor should, and out of the eighty or so people I spoke with that night, at least five asked, 'So, how do you like Iowa?'

"Being ignorant of the Idaho-Iowa connection at the time, I kept wondering why people would ask me how I liked a state I had only passed through. This experience was my first inkling that the two states might be interchangeable in people's minds.

"When our visit in Indiana ended, my husband and I returned to Idaho. That's right, Idaho. I hadn't been back at work two minutes when one of my co-workers asked, 'So ... how was Iowa?' "

In the fall of 1987, officials toured the country in search of items to place in a Martin Luther King time capsule. The official who toured Idaho placed his foot in his mouth.

Before a crowd of dignitaries in Boise, the visitor politely accepted a state seal from Idaho Governor Cecil Andrus. Then, with television cameras recording his words for posterity, the guest intoned:

"Thank you, governor. And I want you to know that the only state seal included in the Martin Luther King time capsule will be this great seal of the state of Iowa."

Carl Hayden, Jackpot, Nevada, wrote:

"Engaged literary agent in New York by telephone.

"At the time, was living in Idaho Falls, Idaho.

"Mailed him three stories. Never heard a word from him next two months, so contacted him."

The agent told Hayden he had sent him a letter containing the good news that all three stories had sold. The agent, however, had made the fatal mistake. The postal service accordingly returned the letter, stamped "No such address."

The address on the envelope was in "Idaho Falls, Iowa."

"Questioned," Hayden continued, "the agent's secretary said she thought Idaho was a misspelling for Iowa.

"By that time, all the deadlines had passed. Missed sales of all three scripts.

"Discontinued agent."

Iowa Senator Tom Harkin discovered the pitfalls of name identification during his 1992 campaign for the Democratic presidential nomination.

A candidate with both courage and a sense of humor, Harkin strode boldy into the quagmire of Iowa-Idaho confusion by being one of the few primary candidates to actually campaign in Idaho.

On a campaign stop in Boise, he admitted the problem was bigger than any candidate.

"I go all over the country," he told his audience, "and I'm invariably introduced as Senator Tom Harkin of Idaho."

The late Idaho Senator Frank Church, who also campaigned for the Democratic presidential nomination, had the same problem in reverse. Everyone thought he was from Iowa.

There has never been a president from Idaho; Iowa has produced only one — Herbert Hoover.

The father of Depression.

Idaho probably took the rap.

Pat Thornton was lying on a beach in Mexico.

"Where are you from?" a curious Canadian asked.

"Boise, Idaho," she replied.

"Oh, really?" the Canadian said, looking bewildered. "How far is that from Davenport?"

When David Day needed a government document available through the U.S. Government Printing Office, he asked his secretary to call the superintendent of documents in Washington, D.C.

The bureaucrat who took the call was sorry to inform the secretary that there was no federal government bookstore in Boise. He did have a suggestion, however. If Day couldn't do without the document, he should try the government bookstore in the nearest large city.

"Which is closer?" he asked. "Chicago or Detroit?"

Seattle, actually. Or San Francisco, Denver, Los Angeles...

Carl Bianchi, administrative director of Idaho's court system, was surprised to learn, late in 1987, that he had been appointed "the Judicial Administration Division Lawyers Conference state representative for Iowa."

"I don't want to toot my own horn," Bianchi wrote, "but to my knowledge, this is the first time that anyone from Idaho has ever been chosen for such an honor.

"I must admit that when I first received the letter, I thought perhaps it could be just another bizarre example of the type of confusion that has been generated by the states of Idaho and Iowa over the years — two states which everyone talks about, but no one has ever seen. But upon further reflection, I realize this is a very clever attempt by the American Bar Association to shake up the system by appointing representatives who do not have any conflicts of interest in their states. Certainly, I would have no reason to try to cover up any of the deficiencies of Iowa lawyers. Further, the more I thought about it, the more I realized that

I was qualified to be Iowa's representative. After all, I have been to Iowa and know generally where it is, and have visited two of Iowa's most famous landmarks: the Sue Bee Honey Plant, and the Piggly Wiggly Grocery Store in Sioux City.

"I intend to take my responsiblities as Iowa's representative very seriously. I will be calling a meeting in Boise soon to discuss my plans, and will probably invite the Iowa Supreme Court ... In the meantime, if you have any ideas about how to improve the operations of the American Bar Association, please feel free to send them to me. I will be glad to forward them to Idaho's state representative, who lives in Bismarck."

Not many Americans can claim to have called both Iowa and Idaho home. One of those courageous individuals is Peggy Bear, a longtime Iowan who moved to Idaho in 1986.

"After many remarks about Idaho being Iowa, etc., the most memorable incident occurred one evening in a store in Boise," she recalled. "As I was showing the checkout girl my driver's license (which still happened to be an Iowa license), I watched as this very innocent looking young lady proceeded to check the license. In doing so, she noticed it was an out-of-state license and said, 'Oh, you're from *Iowa*. Is that like in *Ohio*?'

"Trying to remain as straight-faced as I possibly could, I explained to her where Iowa is, but I don't think she ever quite caught on.

"When we were preparing to move to Idaho from Iowa, people would ask where it was and what part of Iowa it was in. I'm just glad we were able to find it."

Linda Ruppel lives in Idaho but went to college in Iowa. After graduating from a Virgina dental school, she went to the University of Iowa for postgraduate work, then began a practice in Eagle, Idaho — where she regularly receives mail addressed to Eagle, Iowa; Iowa City, Idaho, etc.

Her response to the confusion: personalized automobile license plates with the name of the nation's newest state — IDAWA.

Mike Deupree, a columnist with the *Cedar Rapids Gazette*, has spent his entire life in Iowa — except for four years when he worked for a small newspaper in eastern Idaho.

"I never got the point across to the people there that I wasn't from Ohio," he said. "I kept telling them they really lived in Utaho, so I guess fair is fair."

In frustration, Deupree returned to Iowa, secured a berth on a newspaper there, and spent his idle moments ruminating on possible explanations for the mixups.

He presently decided that, "the reason nobody can keep the two states straight is that nobody gives the slightest damn about either, which all things considered is fine with me. Who cares what people in those weenie little states like Rhode Island think anyway?"

While living in Spain, Francis Bohlin of Emmett, Idaho, met a couple from Hawaii. They became friends and remained in touch for many years. When the couple retired and moved to Arizona (the snowbird instinct apparently is strong enough that even Hawaiians are compelled to winter in Arizona), they sent Bohlin a letter containing the following morsel:

"I've lost your letter, so I won't be able to answer it. Tell me about Emmett, Idaho. Is it a suburb of Des Moines? You mention going to Des Moines. I don't know anything about that part of the U.S. We've lived in the North and South, but never in the West."

The couple was well-educated. She wrote for a New York newspaper; he was a department head at a Hawaiian school.

Presumably not the geography department.

Why fight it?

Teresa Green of Jefferson, Iowa, has had it with conversations like this one:

"Where are you from?"

"Iowa."

"Oh. That's where they grow potatoes!"

No, they grow corn, actually. I'm from Iowa."

"Ohio?"

"IOWA!"

Oh, Idaho."

Green (with a sigh of resignation) - "Yes, I'm from Idaho."

Idaho State Treasurer Lydia Justice Edwards was attending the Kentucky Derby, where she sat at a table with some Kentucky notables.

By the time the race was over, she had been introduced as the state treasurer of Iowa, the secretary of state of Ohio and the secretary of the U.S. Treasury.

"After enough of these rearrangements, I stopped correcting people," she said. "I just smiled and said hello."

Dennis Lorenson was born and raised in a small town named Akron, Iowa.

The town originally was named Portlandville, but its optimistic residents were certain it would grow to be a big city like Akron, Ohio. So it was only logical that they would give it the same name, serenely oblivious to the complications they were creating for those who would follow.

"In the Air Force, I was stationed at a base near Columbus, Ohio," Lorenson wrote. "Every time I had to have paperwork filled out at the base or at some government agency, they would ask for my place of birth and then not wait for me to say Iowa. Every time, a disgusted clerk would have to go back and erase Ohio from the form. It was amazing that when I was discharged, my household goods were actually delivered to the right state."

A glutton for punishment, Lorenson moved to Idaho in 1988. When he stopped to check in with his new employers, he was wearing a black and gold Iowa Hawkeyes T-shirt, which prompted a fellow employee to ask, "Hey, did you go to school at Moscow, too?"

Moscow is the home of the University of Idaho, whose school colors also are black and gold. Other than that, there are no conspicuous similarities between the Hawkeyes and the Vandals.

Boisean Colleen Hunt wanted to visit all fifty states. The six she hadn't seen were in the Midwest — Kansas, Missouri, and Oklahoma —and the South — Arkansas, Kentucky, and Tennessee. The six are contiguous. Two border Iowa. Only Kansas and Oklahoma are within a thousand miles of Idaho.

In September of 1990, she and her husband set out to bag the missing states. They were browsing at a gift shop in

20

Dodge City, Kansas, when a woman approached and asked her where she lived.

"Idaho," Hunt replied.

"Oh," the woman said. "What are you doing in Kansas?"

"I'm on vacation. We're seeing the six states we've missed so far in our travels."

The woman was obviously bewildered. Her eyes clouded; her brow furrowed.

"But why have you missed the states so close to your own?" she said after a lengthy pause.

Hunt explained that Idaho was in the Northwest, not the Midwest.

"Oh," the woman said, obviously relieved. "I thought you had a strange accent to come from Iowa."

Bob Ruth was attending a firefighters' symposium in Orlando, Florida., where he was asked what city he was representing.

"Boise, Idaho," he replied.

"Were you on duty when the jetliner crashed?"

The question was a reference to national news stories about a then-recent accident.

In Sioux City, Iowa.

Ruth dispensed the standard geography lesson, patiently pointing out the respective locations of Iowa and Idaho.

"Oh," his unimpressed colleague replied when he was finished. "I thought you said you were from Des Moines, Idaho."

Nina Bruce is one of the Iowans who emigrated to Idaho. She spent her Iowa years pointing out that, no, the famous potatoes didn't come from her state; her Idaho years explaining that the tall corn didn't, either.

Dodd Snodgrass is one of the relatively few veterans of reverse migration — from Idaho to Iowa.

A native of Lewiston, Idaho, he moved to Iowa to attend college and liked it well enough to stay in the Midwest.

"I tried to educate as many Iowans as I could about Idaho, and they taught me a lot," he wrote. "Did you know that Iowa is an Indian name for 'one who puts to sleep?' Well, to the untrained eye one might think that means landscape. But it isn't so. I missed mountains like crazy in Iowa, but there are plenty of trees and hills, and even a canyon near Ames. The sky and soil are full of colors. Now Nebraska, there's some sleep-inducing landscape."

Snodgrass now lives in Kansas, an Indian word for "people of the south wind."

Many people, including an uncertain but large number of Idahoans, persist in believing that Idaho is an Indian word meaning "sun comes down the mountain." It's actually a made-up name, earlier rejected by Colorado.

The word "Idaho" doesn't mean a bloody thing.

So we have one state named after nothing at all, another

for its ability to induce sleep.

And we wonder why people can't keep them straight.

Brenda Atkinson, who lives in Sun Valley, Idaho, was vacationing in Washington, D.C., when a cab driver asked where she called home.

"Idaho," she warily replied.

"That's a wonderful state," the driver said.

"You've been there?"

"Oh, yes! My wife and I went through Idaho driving from Virginia to Florida on our last vacation."

A few days later, in Baltimore, she was asked the same question.

"Idaho," she said. "I'm from Idaho."

"Idaho?" the puzzled Baltimorean replied with a frown. "That's funny, you don't have an accent at all. But welcome to the United States."

As if we didn't have enough problems ...

The Associated Press reports that "people who confuse Iowa with Idaho won't be helped by David Hannapel, a researcher from the corn state who hopes to revolutionize the farming of potatoes, Idaho's best-known crop."

Hannapel's pet project: the development of "an improved potato better adapted to Midwestern environmental conditions."

With sufficient research and development, he euphorically predicted that potatoes could become "an alternative crop in Iowa's future."

To that end, Hannapel secured a $150,000 grant.

Some people have no conscience at all.

Marilyn Essex is an Associated Press reporter who moved from Boise to Des Moines. While working in Boise, she called AP's Washington, D.C., library to ask how Idaho's senators, James McClure and Steve Symms, voted on a civil rights bill. She said she was calling from Idaho and mentioned each of the senators by name.

"I don't see them listed," the librarian asked after a long pause. "Are you absolutely sure they're from Iowa?"

Stanley Crowe, a Boise attorney, was missing a volume of the *Idaho Digest*, a volume of case law. The digests are published for each state and periodically updated. Deciding he'd done without the missing volume long enough, Crowe ordered a replacement.

So what did the publishers send him, correctly mailed to his Boise address?

We won't mention any names, but it was the latest volume of case law from another state and included the latest legal findings on corn fraud and hog rustling.

Sharon Parrish, Red Oak, is one of countless Iowans who have had it up to their Cenex caps with potato questions. The confusion is never worse, she says, than when Iowa plays in the Rose Bowl.

"Every time the Hawkeyes play, Iowans have to listen to Californians, and others attending the Rose Bowl activities, ask dumb questions about the potato crop," she said. "It's getting old."

Jeanette Fredericks-Weber, who lives in Fort Dodge, Iowa, has suffered similarly.

"When I was visiting in the East, someone asked me where I was from.

"'Iowa,' I said."

"Oh. Do you live near Cleveland?"

"No, that's Ohio. I'm from Iowa!"

"Hmmm. I suppose you eat a lot of potatoes."

Most Iowa-Idaho confusion is harmless, but some tends to be a tad on the scary side. Just ask Don Gaige.

Gaige's problem began with an ileostomy. It became worse when the company that supplies the bags required after the surgery insisted on sending them to Iowa instead of his home in Idaho.

We aren't talking junk mail here, folks. This is serious confusion.

As Gaige put it, "When supplies run low, you get a little edgy."

Patricia Ball, Caldwell, Idaho, was attending an educational conference in Indianapolis, where she received a nametag that read, "Patricia Bell, Boyse, Id."

Recovering from the surprise of being stuck with the wrong last name and the wrong (non-existent, actually) town, she struck up a conversation with a colleague from New York — who was thrilled to learn she was from Idaho.

"I know all about your state!" he said. "Why, I was in Des Moines just last week!"

This happened.

A Chicago cab driver asked his fare what had brought him to Chicago.

"Baseball. I came to see the Cubs and the Giants in the playoffs."

"Oh. Where are you from?"

"Idaho."

"Really? I drive a lot of people, but I don't get many from Idaho."

"It's out west. A lot of people get it mixed up with Iowa."

The driver laughed heartily.

"Iowa!" he said, practically splitting. "How could anyone mix up Idaho and Iowa?"

"I don't know, but they do it all the time. Sometimes they get it confused with Ohio and Indiana, too."

The driver laughed so hard the cab was shaking.

"I don't believe it!" he said. "How could anybody think Idaho was Ohio or Indiana?"

"Beats me."

A pregnant pause. Then ...

"It's part of California, isn't it?"

The Price-Waterhouse people should know the difference between Idaho and Iowa, shouldn't they? A company reliable enough to be entrusted with the Oscars at least ought to know its way around the country.

Wrong. Susan Berner, who works for the Idaho Department of Administration, tells of a call she could hardly believe from a Price-Waterhouse representative:

"The call was from an executive of Price-Waterhouse in New York. Only he wasn't in New York. He was calling me from the airport to get directions to our office in Boise. I naturally assumed he was calling from the Boise airport.

"Satisfied I had given him clear instructions, I hung up and proceeded to get a cup of coffee. I returned to my office three minutes later to a ringing phone. It was him again. He apologized and said he would probably be late getting here as he was in the 'wrong capital.'

"Now I was confused, of course, as there is only one capital I know of in Idaho. When he said he was in Des Moines, well, you can imagine how hard I was laughing on the inside while trying to maintain a professional composure on the outside. I told him it was all right and that people got us mixed up all the time.

"But I'll never trust the envelopes for the Oscars again."

The only known instance of a person actually moving to Idaho thinking it was Iowa is "The Case of the Misplaced Pilot," Mike Kacmarik.

A pilot for an air-freight company, Kacmarik was attending a refresher course at a company training school in Texas when a friend encouraged him to bid for the company's Des Moines route. Kacmarik thought about it and decided to take his friend's advice.

"When the bid sheet came out, I saw Boise, Idaho, and thought that must be the Des Moines run, so I bid for it," he said. "A week later, they said, 'Mike, you're going to Boise.' I said 'where the heck is Boise?' They had to draw me a map to show me where it was."

By then, there was no turning back. The would-be Iowan moved to Idaho in 1985 and has been there ever since.

"I fell in love with Boise right away," he said. "It's kind of embarrassing how I got here, but now I'm glad it happened."

Do Iowans have to put up with being mistaken for Idahoans?

All the time, says Iowa Governor Terry Branstad.

"People are always saying, 'how's the potato crop coming along out there?' " Branstad grumped.

Are there any physical similarities, previously overlooked geographical likenesses, that could explain the confusion?

"Well, Iowa isn't as flat as people think," its governor said, "but Idaho is definitely steeper. We used to think the highest point in Iowa was a glacial moraine. Then we thought it was the Ocheyedan Mound, and then somebody proved it was actually some farmer's hog lot."

In one way, Iowans have it worse than Idahoans.

"It's more common for us to be confused with Idaho, but

people also get us mixed up with Ohio," Branstad said. "The classic example was President Ford standing right under a sign that said Iowa State University and saying how nice it was to be in Ohio."

The most striking similarity between the nation's most confused states?

"Friendly people," the guv replied. "The problem isn't with Iowa or Idaho. It's the other forty-eight states that need to learn the difference.

"Especially those easterners!"

JUST POP IN

There are any number of ways to get from Idaho to Iowa or Iowa to Idaho, but none are quick or easy. To the average American, this simple fact is endlessly surprising.

You can drive between the Confusion States, if you have the time. In a fast car equipped with a fuzz buster and a keg of Maxwell House, it takes a good two days. The scenery alone — sagebrush, alkalai flats and cornfields the size of some Central American nations — is enough to discourage all but the most intrepid motorist.

You can take the bus, if you don't mind spending an epoch on a sweat-soaked seat next to a drunk accordian salesman and a mother of eight, all under the age of five.

You can fly, if you have the money, but even flying is neither quick nor easy. If you doubt this, try getting a direct flight from Cedar Rapids to Pocatello and see what happens.

Despite all this, most people think travel between Iowa and Idaho is swift and virtually effortless.

"You're moving from Des Moines to Boise? Not to worry. We'll be over for pie and coffee every Saturday."

An exaggeration? You be the judge:

John Nelson was a corporate pilot for a Boise-based industrial company. When his boss told him to find the company a larger plane, he became engaged in the following conversation with an aircraft dealer from Texas:

Dealer - I sure would like to show y'all this airplane, as it is really a beauty.

Nelson - We would like to see it. We're quite interested.

Dealer - Say, I know what I can do. I'm showing the aircraft to another party next week. Why don't I just drop by and show it to y'all?

Nelson - Hey, that sounds great! Where are you showing it?

Dealer - I'm showing it to a client in Kentucky.

Nelson - Kentucky? ... Do you know where Idaho is?

Dealer - Well, uh ... isn't it right up there with Iowa and Indiana and Illinois somewheres?

Nelson - Let me put it this way. How long would it take you to fly from where you are in Texas to Denver in this airplane?

Dealer - About three hours.

Nelson - Okay, you know where Denver is. Just keep heading in the same direction for another three hours and you'll be in Idaho.

Dealer - Son of a buck! Is it *that* far?

The third grade classes at Lake Hazel Elementary School in Meridian, Idaho, were selling popsicles to raise money for a field trip to Boise, where the students planned to see an American Theater for Youth production of the "Wizard of Oz."

At the last minute, the company called to say the show had been canceled. The students were crushed.

Then, the following call from American Theater for Youth:

"We were just wondering," a spokesman said to teacher Eileen Thornburgh.

"Yes ..."

"Well, since the production won't be coming to Boise, after all, we were wondering if you could come to the one in Des Moines."

Thornburgh thanked him just the same. There was no way the kids could sell that many popsicles.

The Curry Koehler family received a Christmas portrait coupon from the J.C. Penney Co., mailed to the Koehlers' correct address in Boise. The coupon was good for discounts on children's photo packages.

To take advantage of the savings, the Koehlers were advised to act promptly.

"Your Pixy photographer will be visiting your town for a few days only," the coupon said. "Bring your little one in during the dates shown."

The dates were December 6-9.

The little one was to be taken to the Penney's store at Riverhills Mall, in Iowa Falls, Iowa.

Sally and Perry Kelley, Weiser, Idaho, are among the countless Idahoans who have received geographically absurd promotional letters from the Reader's Digest Sweepstakes.

The *Reader's Digest* has made its name (and innumerable fortunes) promoting America, Americans, and wholesome American values. If anyone should know the U.S. backwards and forwards, it is the editors of the *Reader's Digest*.

But do they really know America?

When it comes to American geography, the *Reader's Digest* doesn't know any more than the average Joe, which isn't saying a whole lot. For years, its sweepstakes people have been sending out letters demonstrating that their knowledge of American geography is suspect beyond the city limits of Pleasantville. The Kelleys' story isn't merely typical; it is one of hundreds reported by people throughout Idaho:

"We received a letter from Reader's Digest Sweepstakes, informing us that we very possibly could be the winner of $50,000," they wrote. "If our name was drawn, we'd need to be in Pleasantville, New York, on November 4 to pick up our prize.

"And just to make sure we made it, they were going to send a Cadillac limousine to our house at 9:30 on the morning of the fourth to pick us up and chauffeur us to O'Hare International Airport, where a jet would fly us to New York.

"Needless to say, we were thrilled! We wondered if the

limo would be pulling a travel trailer and whether we'd camp at KOAs on our way to Chicago. But since we needed to be in New York by that afternoon, we decided the Caddy must be supersonic."

When Boisean Kathy Wilkins purchased a new stereo, she dutifully went through all of the owner's material, including the list of places where she could go for repairs.

The sole listing for Idaho?

National Audio Service, 319 South Gilbert, Iowa City, ID.

There is, of course, an Iowa City, IA — as well as an Idaho City, ID. Iowa City, ID, however, is definitely off the map.

Makes you wonder, doesn't it? If Wilkins lived in Iowa, would the closest place she could get her stereo fixed be in Idaho City, IA? Or should she just pop in to the mall in Pocatello?

Countless companies, foundations, and so on mail promotional material in which recipients are asked to designate the region of the country where they live. To make it easier on them, the companies group states within regions. The recipient is thereby spared the heavy labor of actually writing down long words like "West" or "Mid-west."

The Cancer Research Foundation of America's survey is typical. Its grouping of states for the Midwest Region — Indiana, Illinois, Wisconsin, Michigan, Minnesota, North Dakota, South Dakota, Ohio, Missouri, Oklahoma, Nebraska, Iowa and (you guessed it) Idaho.

The State of Idaho is trying to prove it isn't part of the Midwest by taking out tourism advertisements in national publications. The ads plug the state's whitewater rafting, skiing, rock-climbing, and other outdoor activities.

Look out, Iowans. It's only a matter of time before Dubuque is overrun by tourists in lederhosen.

MANGLED ADDRESSES

People love to complain about the postal service. The rates are forever increasing, the junk mail is a nightmare, Aunt Astrid's ceramic cat arrived in pieces ...

When it comes to making the best of Iowa-Idaho madness, however, the U.S. Postal Service deserves a medal. Someone in New York can write a letter to someone in Iowa, spell the person's name wrong and address the envelope to a town that doesn't exist in Idaho, and somehow — defying all the odds — the postal service makes the delivery to the correct Iowan.

It happens more often than you think. A lot more often.

This chapter is dedicated to the men and women in postal-service blue, who are overdue for some friendly words. God knows they get enough of the other kind.

When it comes to pinpoint knowledge of the Confusion States, no one is above suspicion. Not even the President of the United States.

Thus we have what would seem to be an inexcusable error in the case of the late Daniel Sayler.

Inexcusable in the forty-eight other states, but not you-know-where.

After Sayler died while serving in the military, his daughter, Delores Sims, received a memorial certificate from a grateful, if geographically bewildered, nation.

"The United States of America honors the memory of Daniel H. Sayler," it said. "This certificate is awarded by a grateful nation in recognition of devoted and selfless consecration to the service of our country in the Armed Forces of the United States."

The certificate was embossed with the presidential seal and signed by President Jimmy Carter.

It was mailed, in an embossed White House envelope, to "Mrs. Deloris Sinis," on "Fuller Way Avenue," in "Pocatello, Iowa 83201."

Ms. Sims, who lives in Pocatello, Idaho, said she was "amazed I ever received the award my father earned. The zip code, the unusual name of Pocatello, and a friendly postman that knew there was a Delores on Fullerway are all that saved the day."

Rick Orr has a postcard that traveled more than 6,000 miles to get from Idaho to California.

Orr lives in St. Anthony, Idaho, but the card was addressed to him in St. Anthony, Iowa. First it went from San Diego to Des Moines, where a creative postal clerk rushed it off to Lake Crystal, Wisconsin. (Cliff Claven has nothing on this guy.)

After mystifying postal workers in Wisconsin, the card made yet another cross-country trek, this time to White Bird, Idaho. From there, it was back to (you guessed it) Iowa.

The card, which was mailed May 9, arrived at Orr's

home in St. Anthony on June 26. It was accompanied by a handwritten note from an Iowa postmaster:

"Looks like you're having some trouble getting your postcard."

Leave it to a postmaster to get right to the heart of things.

Joyce Kramer, Ph.D., an associate professor at the University of Minnesota, addressed a request for information to "State of Iowa, American Indian Desk, Department of Health, State Capitol, Boise, Idaho."

The letter was delivered to the Idaho Department of Health and Welfare in Boise.

You have to admire that kind of initiative. Not only did Dr. Kramer try to transplant Iowa to the Northwest, she created a whole new state in the process.

Makes you kind of glad you didn't get your Ph.D., doesn't it?

The postal service moves in mysterious ways.

Dr. John Gordon probably wondered why Steve Tucker took so long to pay his bill. The bill was mailed from Gordon's office to Tucker's Boise apartment, a distance of perhaps three miles.

It arrived three weeks later, postmarked Waterloo, Iowa.

Think that one's bad? Consider the case of Dennis Bell and the wandering medical bill.

Bell's Boise office is across the hall from the Idaho Wellness Center, where his doctor's office is located. The address of the doctor's office is 801 Stilson Road, Suite A; Bell's office address is 801 Stilson Road, Suite C.

In May of 1992, his doctor mailed him a bill, addressed to the office across the hall. Most people would have carried it across, but at the going medical rates the doc probably figured a stamp was a good investment.

The bill traveled hundreds of miles to make it to the office a few steps away. It arrived with a postmark from — honest to God — Waterloo, Iowa.

The only possible explanation is that people in Waterloo are so desperate for something to do that they're driving all the way to Idaho and stealing mail.

If you live in Waterloo and read this, do yourself a favor and get out of the house. Live a little. Start having some good, old-fashioned Iowa fun.

Go out for pie and coffee.

Paint the water tower.

Drive to the mall in Des Moines.

These crazed, thrill-seeking trips to Idaho have got to stop.

Lois Collinsworth was surprised to receive a letter to Louis M. Saul in her mailbox.

The envelope had no return address, no postmark. It was addressed to "Louis M. Saul, 317 East End Avenue, Evansdale, Iowa, 50707."

Collinsworth's address at the time was 206 Central Happy Valley, Nampa, Idaho 83601.

"The only resemblance to me or my address was my first name," Collinsworth said.

Louis Saul, you are hereby advised that Lois Collinsworth has your letter, and the following message: The Selective Service is looking for you.

A letter from Walter H. Behanna of Monongahela, Pennsylvania, was mailed to "Route 64, Council Bluffs, Iowa."

That's where it was mailed. It was delivered to Esther Roe, 3440 Pineridge Avenue, Council, Idaho.

Boisean Jim Fernrite was checking into the Best Western Santa Fe Inn in Weatherford, Texas.

"Where are you from?" the desk clerk asked.

"Boise, Idaho," Fernrite replied.

The clerk carefully wrote it down on the check-in slip: "Jim Fernrite, Boize, Iowa."

When Dick Harpt retired from the U.S. Soil Conservation Service, he told his employers to send his retirement checks to the bank where they previously sent his paychecks — Intermountain State Bank, Cascade, Idaho.

No problem, right?

To celebrate his newfound freedom, Harpt jumped in the car and headed for Alaska, a voyage of discovery all retired Idahoans are compelled to make before heading for the great Winnebago in the sky. After six weeks of chasing moose, or whatever it is people do in Alaska, he returned home to Cascade. One of his first stops was his bank.

No retirement checks.

They had been sent to "Intermountain State Bank, Cascade, Iowa."

"I don't know if there's a Cascade, Iowa," Harpt observed, "but if there is, it's for darned sure it doesn't have an Intermountain State Bank."

You never know. Before it was rejected in favor of a hog lot, the highest point in Iowa was thought to be a landmark known as the Ocheyedan Mound. In the right light, some people say it resembles a mountain.

The Americans United Research Foundation should have an adequate knowledge of American geography, shouldn't it?

Of course it should. So should every American with a high school diploma, but ...

The Foundation, headquartered in Silver Spring, Maryland, mailed a letter to "Roger Reynoldson, University of Iowa, Boise Center, 800 Park Boulevard, Boise, Iowa."

Research isn't what it used to be.

Martin Wilhite, who lives in Kuna, Idaho, but received a letter that the University of Oklahoma addressed to him in Kuna, Iowa, has a theory about the confusion.

"Midwest typists," he surmised, "just automatically translate Idaho to Iowa."

"When I moved to Idaho from Ohio, my aunt asked me how things were in Iowa," transplant Chris Lavelle writes. "And now this!"

"This" was a letter from a friend in Minnesota. It was addressed to "Mr. and Mrs. Chris Lavelle, 3611 Anderson Avenue, De Moines (sic), Idaho."

Keith Olander of Ketchum, Idaho, sent a financial-aid application to Wesleyan University, Middletown, Connecticut. The response was mailed to "Keith Olbedo" in "Katchum, Iowa."

Nothing personal, Keith, but you might want to consider a different university.

When he moved to Idaho from Illinois, Jack Lewis' friends reassured him he still could visit because he'd "only be a state away."

Not long after the move, Lewis received a letter that made him question the wisdom of his decision. The letter, from the Greenwich Hospital Association in Greenwich, Connecticut, had traveled an awfully long way to get to Idaho.

A message stamped on the envelope said it had been "Missent to Ireland." A postal worker there, most likely after studying an Atlas with a magnifying glass, had written in large red letters, "U.S.A."

Are you listening, Iowans? You think you've got problems? How would you like to put up with a whole country that started with "I" and was famous for corn famines?

Idaho and Iowa are the Rodney Dangerfield states. They don't get no respect.

Michael Dake, who works at a storage business in Idaho, was stunned by a letter he received at work. The letter, from the Connecticut headquarters of the Uniroyal Tire Co., was correctly addressed to his office in Idaho. The postal service had stamped the following on the envelope:

"Return to Sender. Country of destination must be shown in full, in English, as last line of address for international mail."

Maybe we should rethink that postal-service medal.

UNIVERSITY OF MINNESOTA
DULUTH

Department of Social Work
College of Education and Human Service Professions
220 Bohannon Hall
10 University Drive
Duluth, Minnesota 55812-2496

State of Iowa
American Indian Desk
Dept. of Health
State Capitol
Boise, Idaho

3-1006
Serving the People of California

State of California, Employment Development Department
Box 942880, Sacramento, CA 94280-0001

OFFICIAL BUSINESS
PENALTY FOR PRIVATE USE, $300

IOWA DEPT OF EMPLOYMENT
CATHY BOURNER
317 MAIN
BOISE, IOWA 83735

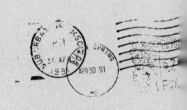

Americans United Research Foundation
900 Silver Spring Avenue
Silver Spring, Maryland 20910

ADDRESS CORRECTION REQUESTED

Mr. Roger Reynoldson
University of Iowa
Boise Center
800 Park Boulevard, Suite 100
Boise, IA 83719

GOOFS IN PRINT

No one is immune to Iowa-Idaho confusion.

No one.

Errors appear in print with unbelievable frequency. Not just mistakes in the church bulletin or the *Mosquito Abatement District Quarterly*; some of the most prominent publications in the land — journals world renowned for their excellence — can't seem to keep Idaho and Iowa straight.

So it's fitting that Idaho-Iowa madness occasioned the first correction ever printed in such a publication — the prestigious *Harper's* magazine.

Think about that. This is a magazine so well written and edited, a magazine whose attention to detail was such a hallmark that in its long and illustrious history it *never needed to run a correction.*

Until Iowa-Idaho came along.

Makes you feel kind of humble, doesn't it?

The fateful error appeared in January, 1986. In a reference to former Idaho Congressman George Hansen, *Harper's* did the citizens of Idaho an inestimable service by identifying him as "George Hansen, R-Iowa." (Hansen was later imprisoned and continues to have trouble with the authorities over money-making schemes. Iowa clearly got the short end of the deal.)

Hansen's unexpected move to Iowa was duly reported in the *Idaho Statesman* in Boise. A few weeks later, a *Harper's* editor called the *Statesman* to report the error had come to her attention and that she and her colleagues were working on a suitable way to report it to their readers. She said it was the first time they had had to run a correction and didn't know how to do it.

The problems some people have! After two months of ruminating on it in God knows how many high-level meetings, *Harper's* got around to publishing a two-sentence correction — and all because of little old Iowa-Idaho.

And you didn't think any of this was serious.

Hansen wasn't the first Idaho congressman to be forcibly transplanted. Idaho's late U.S. Senator Frank Church was identified in the 1972 *Biographical Directory of the American Congress* as having belonged to the Young Democrats of Ohio. The Senate historical office listed him as an Iowan.

This brings us to another respected publication with a geographic Achilles heel, *The Wall Street Journal.*

In 1986, the *Journal's* real-estate section advertised a $450,000 log home for sale in Sun Valley, Iowa.

This was the first known instance in which Sun Valley, the nation's first ski resort, was uprooted to the Midwest rather than California, Colorado, or Utah (where it also isn't, but is often thought to be).

For those uncertain of Sun Valley's location, a hint: it's in a state that begins with "I" and isn't noted for corn, with the exception of its politicians.

The *Journal's* proofreaders should have caught the error when they read that the cabin included a view of snow-capped peaks. In Iowa, the view would have been of Nebraska.

The *Washington Post's* National Weekly Edition of April 8-14, 1991, featured a story on aging populations and dying communities in rural America, specifically Iowa.

The story's dateline was Hedrick, Iowa. It was accompanied by a photograph of downtown Hedrick and included quotes from Hedrick residents. The piece purportedly was about rural America, but the setting was entirely within Iowa. The story was filled with phrases such as, "Iowa towns with populations of less than 500," "farm villages in the Corn Belt," and trips "to Des Moines to the mall."

Smack in the middle of all this Iowa-ness was a quote from Harley Johansen, chairman of the geography department at the University of ... Idaho.

Johansen was correctly identified. He is a department head at the University of Idaho.What was he doing in the middle of a story about Iowa?

Maybe he got lost on the way to the mall.

A story published May 29, 1992, in the painstakingly accurate *New York Times* correctly identified the second-place winner of the Sixty-fifth National Spelling Bee as 14-year-old Erik Wallace of Blackfoot, Idaho.

An accompanying photo caption identified him as a resident of Blackfoot, Iowa.

Iowa-Idaho confusion isn't limited to illustrious publications. The November 14, 1989, edition of the *Star,* a tabloid newspaper, carried a story about a family whose furniture and possessions were taken to a city dump "after zealous city officials found an unkempt lawn."

The city named in the *Star's* report: good old Blackfoot, Iowa.

There is no Blackfoot, Iowa. Blackfoot, Idaho, however, is the home of the Idaho World Potato Exposition. The town modestly bills itself as the potato capital of the world.

It also has some incredibly tidy lawns.

Blackfoot again?
The *National Rural Letter Carrier* of June 10, 1989,

reported the retirement of William W. Smith, who "carried the mail on three different routes from the Blackfoot, Idaho, Post Office."

The story was accompanied by a picture of the retiree, captioned "Iowa Carrier Retires."

Bookstore manager Jack Holmes of Ketchum, Idaho, just up the road from Sun Valley, discovered a smashing example of Iowa-Idaho confusion while reading Robert Ludlum's novel, *The Icarus Agenda.*

Early, Ludlum describes his character Lang Jennings as "a senator from Idaho ... tall and attractive, with a smile that had not been seen since Eisenhower and Shirley Temple." (Ike and Shirley were often confused; they looked so much alike when smiling.)

By page 464, Jennings had become "a farmer from Iowa whose family made a few bucks because his daddy happened to buy 48,000 acres in the mountains that developers sold their souls for."

The Iowa Rockies, perhaps.

Two hundred pages later, Jennings magically returned to his former role as "Lang Jennings from Idaho."

When Holmes brought the discrepancy to the attention of Random House, the book's publishers, he was asked, "Isn't it possible that he could have been from both states? I mean, they are right next door and all. Couldn't his farm have been in the mountains of Iowa and he just crossed over the state line to Idaho?"

Most Iowa-Idaho blunders are merely embarrassing. At least one was criminal.

The *Honolulu Star-Bulletin* of September 7, 1990, reported the demise of a bad-check passer whose undoing was as much geographic as it was underhanded.

The thief was apprehended after a clerk noticed his checks were drawn on the "First Bank of Iowa, Boise, Iowa."

He probably wondered why he got caught.

Some Iowa-Idaho goofs in print are so obvious you wonder how they could possibly happen. In this regard, it's hard to beat a story in the *Columbus* (Indiana) *Republic* of April 5, 1987.

The subject was a legislative effort to remove the "Famous Potatoes" slogan from Idaho's automobile license plates. The story was correctly datelined "Boise, Idaho," and was accompanied by a photograph of J.R. Simplot, the Idaho Potato King, seated at a display of Idaho license plates. The word "Idaho" was clearly visible on each plate.

Beneath the photo was the caption: "Iowa license plates have proudly praised the spud since 1947."

The headline: "License plate issue hot potato in Iowa."

You can't go downhill-skiing in a state that doesn't have ski hills, right?

Not according to *Modern Maturity* magazine, which in its December, 1990-January, 1991 issue told readers of some truly unbelievable ski bargains.

"Several states will help you learn to ski free this winter," MM reported. "From December 15 through 21, novices can receive one day of free lift tickets, equipment rental, and lessons at participating ski areas in Connecticut, Maine, Massachusetts, New Hampshire, and Vermont.

"... Many other states are also offering learn-to-ski packages, either free or for $25 or less. Check out California, Colorado, Iowa ..."

The story didn't say which Iowa ski area was participating. The smart money is on Merrill Sterler's hog lot.

Cutline in the *San Antonio* (Texas) *Express-News*:

"Bonnie Johnson and her husband, Gordon, fly from their boat during a run up the Snake River at the World Jet Boat Championships in Lewiston, Iowa."

Of course! Everyone knows that Iowa is a mecca of whitewater jet-boating. It's what Iowans do to relax after a hard day on the ski slopes.

National magazines in recent years have discovered the benefits of regional advertising, in which advertisers that can't afford national rates purchase local ads in regional editions. Thus we find pitches for Bubba's Diesel Mechanic Institute in *Time*, fundraising appeals for Dunghill Normal School in *Newsweek*, etc.

Sports Illustrated uses the regional approach to promote major league baseball. Readers around the country receive special inserts containing schedules and ticket information for teams in the regions where they live.

The 1990 insert sent to Idaho subscribers was for the Minnesota Twins.

Minnesota shares a border with Iowa, but is more than a thousand miles from Idaho.

The closest major league team to Idaho is the Seattle Mariners.

Maybe the Minnesota offer wasn't so bad.

No feature or department of a publication is safe from the Iowa-Idaho trap. Not even crossword puzzles in newspapers.

In July of 1990, newspapers across the country published a syndicated crossword puzzle using the clue, "Boise bloke." The correct response, according to the syndicate, was "Iowan."

The error came to the attention of Mason City (Iowa) *Globe-Gazette* Editor Jim Kelsh, via a letter from Marian McDonald, a frustrated Iowa reader.

"We Iowans are often amused, and sometimes annoyed, when our state is confused with Idaho," McDonald wrote. "Now comes the Sunday crossword puzzle giving the clue 'Boise bloke,' for which the solution, you would think, would be 'Idahoan.' But no, it is, unbelievably, 'Iowan.'"

Believe it, Marian. It happens all the time.

Marian felt compelled to report the error to the syndicate.

"My call went to a courteous gentleman in New York," she reported. "I identified myself and told him I had a problem with the puzzle. He took a few moments to get the puzzle and then I directed him to 84 Down.

"'You ask for a Boise bloke,' I said, 'but your answer is Iowan.'"

The response was a long pause, followed by a single word:

"So?"

Ah, New Yorkers!

McDonald, a crossword-puzzle junkie, tells yet another story of confusion between the states.

"I have a rather upscale crossword-puzzle book published by Running Press of Philadelphia," she writes. "This book, titled *Crosswords # 14*, edited by Mel Rosen, says prominently on the cover: Guaranteed! These puzzles have been proofread and cross-checked six times to insure accuracy.

"In puzzle number ten of the book, clue 63 Down is: Coeur d'_____, Iowa. The answer that fits is, of course, 'Alene.' There is obviously no city of that name in Iowa as there is in Idaho.

"I wrote to the publisher inquiring about the guarantee. Remuneration? Free book? Mea culpa?

"Of course, no response."

People magazine, in an investigative story in 1987 about a grievance against the J.R. Simplot Co., ended the piece with the words, "She left Iowa and now resides in Oregon."

She didn't leave Iowa. She left Idaho, which is adjacent to Oregon, the home of the J.R. Simplot Co., and the setting for the dispute that inspired *People's* story.

The report was a departure from *People's* usual style, which may have accounted for the mixup. The editors were probably preoccupied with photos of Madonna on a Davenport.

Quilting Today publishes a list of upcoming events for quilters. Under a bold headline reading "Idaho," was an event listed as "Quilt Extravaganza III, March 28 to April 1, 1990; Fifteenth and Woodland, Des Moines."

April Fool!

The *Chronology and Documentary Handbook of the State of Idaho* (who says there isn't a cure for insomnia?) prefaces an article about a country teacher by describing it as "a fine discussion of the country schools as developed in Page County, Idaho."

Immediately following is a headline, "Country Schools for Country Children." Immediately following that are the words, "The simple motto by which Miss Jessie Field has made a wonderful transformation in education in Page County, Iowa."

Miss Field got around, didn't she?

UNIX Today, a magazine for computer users, lists the location of its Idaho seminars as Boise and Des Moines.

Beneath an Idaho headline in its "News from Around the U.S.A." section, *USA Today* reported the appointment of President George Bush's ninety-fourth point of light, in Boise, and a murder by strangulation in Davenport.

When Henry Kissinger did a stint as a guest weatherman on CBS This Morning, he was pictured in a wire-service photo, aiming a pointer at a weather map.

An accompanying cutline reported that the former Secretary of State and the program's regular weatherman were "discussing the location of Idaho."

The pointer was aimed squarely at Iowa.

The Loneliest Campaign: the Truman Victory of 1948, by Irwin Ross, reports that the former President had "sufficient strength to win some Midwestern states; in the end, Truman took Idaho, Iowa, Minnesota, Missouri, and Wisconsin, as well as Ohio and Illinois."

So what about the other "I" state — Indiana?

Probably too far west to be worth mentioning.

QST, a magazine for radio buffs, ran a series of briefs congratulating radio amateurs on their years as members of an amateur radio league. Among those congratulated for fifty years of service was Robert S. Reynolds, of "Waterloo, Idaho."

A logical mistake. Waterloo, Iowa, is where Boise's mail goes.

The Attleboro, Massachusetts, *Sun Chronicle* of August 7, 1992, featured a front-page photo of Bill Clinton speaking to a large crowd during his campaign for the presidency.

The cutline beneath the photo read, "Bill Clinton addresses crowd in Strawberry Point, Idaho, on Democratic bus tour."

Clinton was in Strawberry Point, Iowa.

A 1987 advertisement in *Runner's World* gave each state's race locations for the Pepsi 10,000-meter Race.

The starting locations for Idaho were all in Iowa.

That's one hell of a footrace.

CANADIAN WESTERN NATURAL GAS
COMPANY LIMITED
909 - ELEVENTH AVENUE S.W., CALGARY, ALBERTA T2R 1L8

Iowa Power Company
Fred Todd
P.O. Box 70
BOISE, Ohio
U.S.A.
83707   D

NEW JERSEY & YOU PERFECT TOGETHER

10/29

Scott Whipp
11665 W. Freedom Dr.
Bois, Ohio 83704

w3,coe,fmt,nap

60

RADIO AND TV

One of the great advantages of electronic journalism over print is that of the fleeting image.

Broadcasters can make mistakes print journalists would be flogged for and no one notices, courtesy of the all-forgiving fleeting image. Now you see it, now you don't. Now you hear it ... or did you?

Dan Rather can identify Baby Jessica, the child who riveted the nation by falling down a well, as "little Jessica Hahn," and the viewers blithely sail through their TV dinners, oblivious to the atrocity. (Jessica Hahn, for those who have forgotten, was the off-screen playmate of ex-television evangelist Jim Bakker.) A print journalist would be crucified in the "Letters to the Editor" column for a mistake like that, but broadcast journalists are uniquely immune.

Well, almost. Iowa-Idaho watchers are forever on the alert for pet atrocities, on the air as well as in print. Thus this small, but gratifying, chapter:

Sharon Pipes, an Idaho transplant living in Nevada, was treated to a fine specimen of confusion on the evening news on Channel Four in Reno.

The local anchorman, she reports, was holding forth on the subject of riverboats. The boats that had caught his fancy were in Iowa, presumably on the Iowa River. There was no way of being certain, however, as it alternately was identified as the Iowa River and the Ohio River. Not wishing to leave anyone out, the announcer thoughtfully threw in "Idaho River" from time to time, as a courtesy. (Television announcers tend to interchange the "I" states and Ohio at will.)

Later in the same newscast, Idaho Congressman Larry Craig was identified as an Ohio Republican.

Residents of the small town of Melba, Idaho, had mixed feelings when a local girl, Renee Tenison, was named *Playboy* magazine's Playmate of the Year for 1989.

Some Melbans considered the honor a dubious one. Others argued that Tenison's recognition would put their town in the limelight.

It did, too

Sort of.

No one was more surprised than Tenison herself when, on the night of April 26, 1990, CNN's Barry Judge identified her as a native of the small town of Melba, Iowa.

CNN, acclaimed for its round-the-clock coverage of the Persian Gulf War, stubbed its toe again while reporting a relatively routine story about spring floods in the Midwest.

The story was detailed and accurate, with one exception. Near the end of the report, CNN's corrrespondent solemnly announced that Governor Cecil Andrus was giving serious consideration to declaring part of Ohio a disaster area.

Ohio Governor George Voinovich probably wasn't too happy about that. Andrus is the Governor of Idaho.

The "MacNeil-Lehrer Report" of October 23, 1989, created a modest stir in Idaho by reporting that one of its U.S. senators had changed states.

An interview with Idaho Senator Steve Symms began with his introduction as Senator Steve Symms of Iowa.

To Idahoans still smarting from a recent report that Symms had infuriated the management of a Brazilian luxury hotel by cleaning his muddy boots in a bidet, the change of address wasn't entirely unwelcome.

Anchorpersons, start your blowdryers.

In her report of June 26, 1990, the "Today Show's" Deborah Norville moved Boise to Ohio.

The mistake wasn't without precedent. Tom Brokaw — reporting from Boise — had previously moved it to Iowa.

To her credit, Norville caught and corrected her error. Brokaw didn't, and went on to anchor the "NBC Evening

Brokaw didn't, and went on to anchor the "NBC Evening News."

Brokaw replaced John Chancellor, who was noted for being authoritative and accurate. You don't have to have a pretty face to make it in broadcast journalism, but it doesn't hurt.

Not all of the errors are accidental. Some television programs intentionally contribute to Iowa-Idaho confusion.

One of the earliest examples was the following exchange on "The Patty Duke Show:"

Kid - So where did you move here from?

New kid on the block - Idaho.

Kid - Oh, Iowa?

New Kid - No, Idaho!

Kid - Well, here in Brooklyn, we pronounce it Iowa.

The line was lifted from *The New Yorker,* whose readers aren't noted for being fans of "The Patty Duke Show." It's doubtful anyone noticed.

Another situation comedy, "Who's the Boss?" carried the tradition into the '90s. In its final episode, one of the characters landed a job in Iowa. Faithful to the end, his co-star presented him with a map and charted his course to ... Idaho.

Margaret King was watching the CBS News on Channel Six in Portland, Oregon, on September 6, 1987, when weather announcer Mark McEwen calmly informed her that the high temperature was seventy-four degrees that day in Boise, Ohio.

Larry King succumbed to the madness on February 6, 1991, while interviewing actor Steve Martin about his then-latest movie, "L.A. Story."

The point King was trying to make was that to get the most from the film, it was necessary to have lived in Los Angeles and experienced its eccentricities firsthand. The point was fine, but the execution was flawed.

"You couldn't have made this movie just anywhere," he said. "You don't make a movie like this about Sioux Falls, Idaho."

No argument there, Larry.

Kempthorne had his day in the sun by speaking at the 1992 Republican National Convention, an unexpected cloud darkened the horizon.

The hometown fans' buttons were bursting — until a CNN graphic identified Kempthorne to the rest of the nation.

The graphic: Dirk Kempthorne, U.S. Senate Candidate, R-Indiana.

The error appeared twice before CNN corrected it, on its third and final appearance. By then, the speech was nearly over.

The following is the true story (with minor embellishments) of a National Public Radio interview on one of the significant issues of our time, publication of this book:

"Hello, this is NPR calling. We read about your book on the confusion between Iowa and Idaho and were wondering if you'd be willing to do an interview about it."

"Sure. When did you have in mind?"

"About fifteen minutes from now. We'll have our affiliate in Idaho call you. They'll be the ones doing it. Just a minute ..."

Short pause.

"Hey, Bubba! We do have an affiliate in Idaho, don't we?"

"Yeah. It's in Ames."

The affiliate in Idaho is KBSU, located at Boise State University. Ames is the home of the University of Iowa,

University. Ames is the home of the University of Iowa, which isn't quite the same thing. This was politely explained to NPR's editor, who promised to call back. Ten minutes later, the phone rang again.

"There isn't anyone at our Idaho affiliate who knows how to do the interview," he said. "We're going to do it ourselves."

The interview drew mixed reactions at KBSU. The station had done numerous interviews for NPR and, according to its staff, never was contacted.

Further checking revealed that NPR's request for assistance had gone to its affiliate in ...

Ames.

BELLEVILLE
ECONOMIC PROGRESS, INC.
Serving St. Clair County
216 East "A" Street, Belleville, Illinois 62220-1460 • (618) 233-2015

September 20, 1992

Iowa   Department of Transportation
800 Lincoln Way
Boise, ID 83707

Dear Sir or Madam:

One of the functions of Belleville Economic Progress is to act as the Chamber of Commerce for the City of Belleville. We like to maintain a supply of maps which are requested by the general public.

We no longer have any Iowa maps. Please send us fifty copies of your most recent map.

Your prompt assistance would be most appreciated.

Sincerely,

Patty Rensing
Administrative Assistant

68

SUPPORTING ROLES

Well, yes. Most of the mixups are between Iowa and Idaho.

Not to be left out, however, are other states that happily share in the confusion. Indiana is the most frequent interloper, with Ohio a strong second. But the confusion is by no means limited to "I" states and Ohio. Some highly unlikely guests have been known to crash the Iowa-Idaho party.

To wit:

South Dakota?

Roxanne Overton, who lives in Boise, received an invitation to a spring sale held by the Hartmann Co., which makes handcrafted luggage. It was surprising she received it at all.

Overton's correct address was: Roxanne Overton, 4955 Bitterbrush Drive, Boise, Idaho.

The invitation was addressed to: Roxanne Quertore, 4955 Biuter Brush, Boise, S.D.

Forget the sale. Where are the invitations to the spring party in the Hartmann mailroom?

Barbara Dorrity tells a similar story. Clement Communications, Inc. sent her a catalog mailed to the dubious address of "Barbara, Parcel Drop, 1902 Vista Avenue, Boise, N.M."

Boise, New Mexico?

Dorrity doesn't have a parcel drop and doesn't live on Vista Avenue. The only correct part of the address was the city. Barbara does live in Boise.

The one in Idaho.

Bob Gholson has the distinction of being a key figure in a plot to move Idaho's capital to Wisconsin.

In 1988, Gholson received an AT&T data processing requisition mailed to his address in "Boise, Wisconsin," complete with a Wisconsin zip code.

"It seems that after over a year of receiving regular billing statements from AT&T, they have seen fit to move me to the Midwest," he said. "Iowa I could understand, but Wisconsin? Not only that, they also now have me living at an address we moved from in mid-1986."

In typically heroic fashion, the postal service delivered the requistion to Gholson's new address in Boise, Idaho.

If you really need to reach out and touch someone, send a letter.

Michael Reed, a jeweler, didn't put much stock in geographical confusion until his business cards were printed with the following address: 500 West Idaho Street, Suite 203, Boise, Ohio 83702.

His response: a custom watch featuring "a unique display of Idaho and neighboring states."

That's fine for Idahoans, but what about the East, where most Iowa-Idaho confusion originates? What Reed ought to make is a watch with a face designed for easterners. Oregon, Washington, Nevada, Utah, Wyoming, Montana, and Canada would comprise the rest of the face; Idaho would be Mickey's nose.

Chris Andrew knows how Reed feels. His business cards identify him as the store manager of "Herman's Sporting Goods, 5801 Fairview Avenue, Boise, Ohio."

Is it starting to sound like these things only happen to people in Boise?

Of course it is. That's because the writer has been writing Iowa-Idaho columns appearing in the Boise newspaper for years. If the Des Moines paper had been shrewd enough to pick them up, there'd be lots of Iowa stories here.

You can bet the farm that Iowa towns get moved to Idaho all the time, but you'd never know it — thanks to some Iowa editor who was worrying about the weather map or the latest redesign when he should have had his eye on the truly important things in life. This is mentioned for the benefit of Iowa readers, who will find the going easier knowing there is someone close to home whom they can blame.

Iowans don't like the chaos any better than Idahoans do. Dan Beid, a columnist in West Burlington, Iowa, writes that he is sick and tired of people who think "our capital is Boise and our best football teams are coached by a buffoon named Woody Hayes."

Fred Todd, who works in Boise for Idaho Power Company, couldn't believe it when he received a letter addressed to, "Fred Todd, Iowa Power Company, P.O. Box 70, Boise, Ohio, U.S.A. 83707."

It has a certain beauty, doesn't it? An Idahoan working for an Iowa company in Ohio. If they'd just been able to work in Indiana, it would have been perfect.

On the other hand, at least they had an excuse. The letter was from a company in Calgary, Canada. Most Canadians — this particular letter's author notwithstanding — are remarkably well informed about the U.S. How much does the average Yank know about Canadian geography?

Poor George Hansen.

You recall that it was Hansen, the former Idaho congressman, that *Harper's* moved to Iowa, resulting in the magazine's first-ever correction. Not to be outdone, the *Northwest Florida Daily News* moved Hansen to Indiana.

The error occurred in a listing of congressional reprimands, including Hansen's for "financial misconduct."

To *Harper's* and the *Northwest Florida Daily News*, on behalf of Idahoans everywhere ... thank you.

Folks in Hailey, Idaho, are proud of their most famous native son, poet Ezra Pound. Ezra left Hailey as an infant and never returned, but it doesn't matter. Famous native sons aren't easy to come by in places like Hailey.

So it was a matter of some concern when the "Literary Companion Calendar," published by the New York Public Library, gave Pound's birthplace as "Hailey, Ohio."

Lori Benton, an Idahoan who noticed the error while

working in a bookstore, decided to stop during a visit to New York and inform the authorities at New York Public that they had blown it.

"The initial reaction was disbelief," she said. "The man at the desk told me the calendar had been well researched and was known for being scrupulously accurate. It took some doing to convince him."

His response, once convinced:

"Well, you know it is awfully easy to confuse those Midwest states."

Worth at least passing mention is a town with what would seem to have one of the most confusion-prone names in the United States — Idaho, Ohio.

No, it isn't a joke. Idaho (pronounced I-dee-ho) is a village of approximately seventy-five inhabitants in the rolling hills of southern Ohio. That's the unofficial population according to Idaho native Blaine Beekman, town historian and the mayor of nearby Waverly, Ohio, the county seat. Idaho doesn't have a mayor.

"Let's see, a couple of houses burned down and they moved a trailer, so I guess there must be about seventy-five people now," he said.

"None are from the state of Idaho. If there is a connection, no one knows what it is.

"I don't know, and no one else around here does, either," Beekman said. "I often ask about it. It's been around as a village since about 1870, but there's no record of how it got its name."

Despite the confusion potential, Beekman says mixups are virtually non-existent.

"There's no railroad and only one highway," he said. "No tourists come through, and the natives never give Idaho much thought. We'd be pleased if there was confusion. That would be a big event in Idaho."

Idaho the village preceded Idaho the state, which wasn't admitted to the Union until 1890.

"We think the state was probably named after us," Beekman said.

If you drive an Edsel, you should be ready for anything, right?

But there was no way Dave Ward could have been ready for his insurance company's response to his request to have his car reinsured.

Ward is a member of an Edsel owners' club in Nampa, Idaho. When it was time to reinsure, an unusually long delay was followed by a letter from the company.

If the letter had said the car was too old, Ward would have been ready with an argument.

If the letter had said his car was too weird, he'd have been ready to fight.

Instead, the letter said the delay had been caused by technicalities the company had had to research with regard to the insurance laws of Indiana.

The Edsel, it added, would be subject to extra charges

rising from "special provisions of Indiana state law."

The letter didn't say whether there were any special provisions of Idaho law applicable to Hoosiers.

Editors working for "Aware," an organization for wine enthusiasts, may have had one too many when they compiled a 1990 list of new members. In it, Idaho winemakers Gail Jensen and Mimi Mook were transplanted to Indiana.

"We both were amused by it," Jensen wrote, "but we also both wrote them to ask them to correct the error. It is especially ridiculous for Mimi because Ste. Chapelle is the biggest winery in Idaho."

Which is a little like saying the biggest creamery in Arizona. If Ste. Chapelle were Idaho's biggest spuddery, now *that* would have been ridiculous.

Idaho has the largest wilderness area in the contiguous forty-eight states, but you wouldn't know it from reading "Corporate Views of the Public Interest; Perceptions of the Forest Products Industry," by Jeffrey Sonnefeld.

The book reports that, "President Carter signed into law the creation of the 2.2 million-acre River of No Return Wilderness in central Ohio, the largest wilderness area in 49 states exceeded only by the Alaskan wilderness."

All that wilderness must have gone to Sonnefeld's head.

Some incredibly smart people work for the Hewelett-Packard company. The company makes sophisticated electronics products and is not noted for employing Bozos.

Except when it comes to geography.

Debby Hampton received a call from Hewlett-Packard about a problem the company was having regarding her husband's computer. Her husband had been having trouble with the computer, which was why he'd asked the company to have a technician drop by and fix it.

HP agreed to have one of its incredibly smart people come and have a look. There was just one, trifling difficulty. None of the company's incredibly smart people was able to find the town where the Hamptons lived — Melba, Idaho — on the map. They said they'd looked and looked, but couldn't find Melba anywhere.

"What map are you looking on?" Debby asked.

The question was followed by an embarrassed silence.

"... You mean it's not on the map of Indiana?"

Gary Glenn wasn't at all surprised to receive a letter from E.I. Du Pont Nemours and Co., in Wilmington, Delaware, addressed to him at the "Ohio Cattle Associates in Boise, Ohio."

At the time, Glenn was working for the Idaho Cattle Associates — in Boise, you-know-where.

Sean Chaney, of Caldwell, Idaho, was a big fan of Sammy Davis, Jr. His letter complimenting Davis on his work and requesting an autographed photo was answered by Treva Wilson, the late entertainer's secretary.

"Mr. Davis thanks you for watching all the television specials," she wrote. "To the best of our knowledge, no movie is being made with Mr. Davis and Jonathan Winters. Mr. Davis will be touring with Frank Sinatra and Dean Martin this year; unfortunately no show is planned for Indiana."

Nothing if not consistent, Wilson addressed the letter to Caldwell, Indiana. It didn't say whether any shows were planned for Idaho.

Sarah Nott eagerly scanned her latest issue of *Front and Finish*, a newspaper for dog fanciers, to see whether her friend Alta Seltz was listed as a new member.

She was, all right. There was Alta's name, listed as the proud owner of "Alta's Schoenste Von Ebony," a Rottweiler. Dog and master were shown as residing in Kuma, Indiana.

There is no Kuma, Indiana.
Seltz lives in Kuna, Idaho.

During a visit to the now defunct Soviet Union, Boisean Vi Walker was startled to learn that she was listed on the airline passenger manifest as being from Boise, Ohio.

Her daughter was listed as a resident of Kuna, Indiana.

Teri Thompson was thrilled when she won honorable mention in a knitting contest sponsored by *Decorating and Remodeling* magazine.

The thrill was tempered by the magazine's announcement of her achievement, complete with her hometown of "Idaho Falls, Indiana."

Come on, editors! Let's get a grip here. Idaho Falls, Indiana? Shouldn't something about that sound a warning bell? How many waterfalls are there in Indiana? And even if there are waterfalls in Indiana, what kind of weirdo would name one in honor of Idaho?

Whatever happened to reference books? Whatever happened to the lost art of geography? Whatever happened to editors with green eyeshades and an abiding hatred for the careless error?

Idaho Falls, Indiana? What the hell is the world coming to?

Mike Arbanas, an Idaho newspaper reporter, was having dinner when the nightly telephone-solicitation call (why do they always call at dinnertime?) interrupted his meal.

"Mr. Arbanas?"

"Yes?"

"I'm calling on behalf of the Indiana Special Olympics."

"Really? I don't know much about the Indiana Special Olympics. I live in Idaho."

"That isn't a problem, Mr. Arbanas. The program is statewide."

Even the postal service has its lapses. A 1987 news release from the Cattlemen's Beef Promotion and Research Board in Englewood, Colorado, was addressed to, "Editor, State Journal-Register, P.O. Box 219, Springfield, Illinois."

It was delivered to the *Idaho Statesman* in Boise.

A mere 1,700 miles off.

Nobody's perfect.

You thought we were joking about new states and cities being created? In Boise, it happens all the time.

The Boise office of the Zellerbach paper company received an order addressed to "Blaise, Indiana."

P.J. Laws was surprised to arrive at her office one morning and find a package addressed to her at "KTVB Television, Boyse, Iowa."

When Orville Clark wrote to a California company about buying a part for his mobile home, the response was addressed to "DeMois, Iowa." It somehow arrived (take another bow, postal workers) at his Boise home.

The Department of Health and Human Services in Atlanta sent Joy Hummel of the Idaho Department of Education a letter addressed to "Biose, Idaha."

The New Jersey Division of Travel and Tourism — of all people — sent Scott Whipp a packet addressed to "Bois, Ohio."

Boisean Margie Mulby received a letter mailed to her home address in "Bosie, Odaho."

And Sally Segel of the Ada County Sheriff's office in Boise could hardly keep from laughing during a call from someone who just had to speak with "the sheriff of Boise, Ohido."

Who says Yankee ingenuity isn't what it used to be?

THE WHITE HOUSE

wrong address

MRS. DELORIS SINIS
135 FULLER WAY
POCATELLO, IA 83201

do not bend